GW00360392

ASTROLOGY GEMS

SCORPIO
October 23 – November 21

Monte Farber & Amy Zerner

®
Sterling Publishing Co., Inc.
New York

Text © 2006 by Monte Farber
Art © 2006 by Amy Zerner

10 9 8 7 6 5 4 3 2 1

Published by Sterling Publishing Co., Inc.
387 Park Avenue South, New York, NY 10016

Distributed in Canada by Sterling Publishing
c/o Canadian Manda Group, 165 Dufferin Street
Toronto, Ontario, Canada M6K 3H6

Distributed in the United Kingdom by GMC
Distribution Services
Castle Place, 166 High Street, Lewes, East Sussex,
England BN7 1XU

Distributed in Australia by Capricorn Link (Australia)
Pty. Ltd.
P.O. Box 704, Windsor, NSW 2756, Australia

Printed in China

Sterling ISBN-13: 978-1-4027-4184-5
          ISBN-10: 1-4027-4184-7

For information about custom editions, special sales,
premium and corporate purchases, please contact
Sterling Special Sales Department at 800-805-5489 or
specialsales@sterlingpub.com.

What's Your Sign?

When someone asks you "What's your sign?" you know what that person really means is "What's your astrological sign?" Professional astrologers more often use the phrase "Sun sign," a term reflecting the concept that a person's sign is determined by which of the twelve signs of the zodiac the Sun appeared to be passing through at the moment she was born. The zodiac is the narrow band of sky circling the Earth's equator through which the Sun, the Moon, and the planets appear to move when viewed by us here on Earth.

Astrology's Gift

Astrology, which has been around for thousands of years, is the study of how planetary positions relate to earthly events and people. Its long and rich history has resulted in a wealth of philosophical and psychological wisdom, the basic concepts of which we are going to share with you in the pages of this book. As the Greek philosopher Heracleitus (c. 540–c. 480 BCE) said, "Character is destiny." Who you are—complete with all of your goals, tendencies, habits, virtues, and vices—will

determine how you act and react, thereby creating your life's destiny. Like astrology itself, our Astrology Gems series is designed to help you to better know yourself and those you care about. You will then be better able to use your free will to shape your life to your liking.

Does Astrology Work?

Many people rightly question how astrology can divide humanity into twelve Sun signs and make predictions that can be correct for everyone of the same sign. The simple answer is that it cannot do that—that's newspaper astrology, entertaining but not the real thing. Rather, astrology can help you understand your strengths and weaknesses so that you can better accept yourself as you are and use your strengths to compensate for your weaknesses. Real astrology is designed to help you to become yourself fully.

Remember, virtually all the music in the history of Western music has been composed using variations of the same twelve notes. Similarly, the twelve Sun signs of astrology are basic themes rich with meaning that each of us expresses differently to create and respond to the unique opportunities and challenges of our life.

SCORPIO

October 23–November 21

Planet
Pluto

Element
Water

Quality
Fixed

Day
Tuesday

Season
autumn

Colors
black, dark red, maroon

Plants
gardenia, rhododendron, anemone

Perfume
tuberose

Gemstones
agate, onyx, ruby, obsidian

Metal
plutonium

Personal qualities
Intense, obsessive, loyal, determined,
and passionate

KEYWORDS

We call the following words "keywords" because they can help you
unlock the core meaning of the
astrological sign of Scorpio. Each
keyword represents issues and
ideas that are of supreme importance and prominence in the lives
of people born with Scorpio as
their Sun sign. You will usually find
that every Scorpio embodies at
least one of these keywords in the
way he makes a living:

investigation · wills and taxes
secrets · profundity · intuition
sexual politics · mysteries
good detective · transformation
power play · transcend
resurrect · legacy · regenerate
absolute · conscience · exchange
labyrinth · control · obsession
precision · purify · subterfuge
death and transfiguration · clues
research · enemies list · judge
underground tunnel · recycling
psychology · reincarnation

Scorpio's Symbolic Meaning

Scorpio is the master detective of the zodiac. If there's something or someone Scorpio wants to know about, nothing and no one can prevent her from discovering the hidden truth. It is as if she feels compelled to know all the secrets just in case she needs to use them to prove how powerful she is.

When it comes to their own secrets, Scorpios are equally skilled at keeping them from others. In this way they prevent others from having power over them. They rarely volunteer information, for the same reason. Power in all its forms is one of the biggest issues for Scorpios to deal with. Most elements of life are imbued with overtones of power for Scorpio, including money, sex, authority, and knowledge. Most Scorpios are powerful and know it. However, if a Scorpio doubts her own power, she becomes so attracted to it that she is willing to do practically anything to get it. This can obviously put her in intense situations.

Most Scorpios are as fearless as their most well-known symbol, the Scorpion. But like a scorpion, they can be so intent on stinging something that they end up stinging themselves. Their intensity is such that other people can't believe that they really mean what they are saying. Scorpios are often misunderstood because of the intensity of their passion. The other symbol for this sign is the Phoenix, which rises in triumph from its own ashes. This archetype symbolizes the extremes to which the sign is typically drawn.

Scorpio is one of the four Fixed Sun signs in astrology (the other three are Taurus, Aquarius, and Leo). Fixed signs are associated with stability and determination. Concentration, focus, consolidation, and perseverance are all hallmarks of a fixed Sun sign. Scorpio is the Fixed Water sign of the zodiac. It is one of three Water signs in the zodiac (the other two are Pisces and Cancer). Water is the element that makes a Scorpio emotional, sensitive, feeling, and hidden. In the case of Scorpio, still waters do run deep.

The lesson for Scorpios to learn is that there is an important reason that their life does not provide them with as many peak experiences as they would like. They have come into this world with the astrological sign Scorpio because they want to learn how to develop their ability to work their powerful will on the world. The sign Scorpio rules magic, and Scorpios want to make big changes in their lives, the kinds that appear to other people as almost magical transformations.

Recognizing a Scorpio

People who exhibit the physical characteristics distinctive of the sign of Scorpio
have strong features, attractive looks,
thick hair and eyebrows, and eyes with an
almost hypnotic intensity. A Scorpio is
inclined to point his head down. Even in
repose, Scorpio's expression remains
intense. When looking directly at a
person, a Scorpio makes his subject feel
penetrated. A Scorpio, even when
slender, can have a rather thick waist.

Scorpio's Typical Behavior and Personality Traits

- loyal to family and home
- intensely loyal to friends
- passionate about beliefs
- never forgives or forgets
- relentless about winning
- flirts only when seriously interested
- has very high standards
- can be a saint or a sinner

- has to maintain his dignity
- is a force to be reckoned with
- very brave under adversity
- gives ruthlessly honest advice
- pursues interests with great zeal
- can be quite secretive
- will work behind the scenes

What Makes a Scorpio Tick?

Scorpios are keen students of psychology and always want to know what makes people do the things they do. Compulsions and strange behavior do not faze a Scorpio one bit. In fact, her curiosity is piqued. Undeveloped Scorpios have a tendency to use their intimate understanding of human motivations for ruthless manipulation cunningly designed to attain selfish goals. While Scorpios are constantly trying to uncover the secrets of others, they guard their own privacy with almost manic intensity.

The Scorpio
Personality
Expressed Positively

It is in the nature of Scorpio to pursue an interest or endeavor to its limit, regardless of personal cost or effort. That is how a Scorpio best fulfills his destiny. This is a Sun sign of extremes, and Scorpio often takes his desire for secrecy very seriously, resulting in cordial yet careful relationships.

On a Positive Note

Scorpios displaying the positive characteristics associated with their sign also tend to be:

❀ protective of loved ones

❀ magnetic and dynamic

❀ compassionate and emotional

❀ tenacious and probing

❀ safety conscious

❀ passionate

❀ intense concentrators

❀ sensual

❀ intuitive

The Scorpio Personality Expressed Negatively

A frustrated Scorpio can be a difficult and angry person. Usually this is the result of feeling as if she has a lack of power or a sense that her life is not progressing in the way she hoped. Since it can be hard for an unhappy Scorpio to admit any fault, she has a tendency to blame others for her failures.

Negative Traits

Scorpios displaying the negative characteristics associated with their sign also tend to be:

- ruthless and vindictive
- jealous and possessive
- suspicious
- self-destructive
- intolerant and sarcastic
- obstinate
- secretive
- moody
- insulting

Ask a Scorpio If…

Ask a Scorpio if you want to get to the bottom of a mystery. Their penetrating intelligence and ability to put clues together are a tremendous help. Scorpios also have strong powers of intuition, which helps them to discover truths both minor and major. They are also great judges of character, so it is very hard to fool them in any way. If a Scorpio has advice to give, it is best to listen. They aren't gossips and aren't the sort who spread idle rumors. A Scorpio can carry a secret to his deathbed.

Scorpios As Friends

When Scorpios focus their energies on controlling their friends, they find in the end that they, themselves, end up being under the control of others. However, when they turn their efforts towards self-control, the influence they have on both their friends and the world around them seems to be without bounds. It is as if the best way for them to control a situation is to be in control of themselves.

In general, Scorpio likes a friend who recognizes Scorpio's magnetic and intense personality and appreciates that she is deeply caring and emotionally involved. Scorpio chooses only a few friends and expects loyalty from them. Scorpio keeps close friends for many years.

Scorpios have good memories and enjoy telling jokes. They are generous and hospitable toward friends, and also make strangers welcome when they call for help or advice.

Looking for Love

Despite their passionate nature and need to feel as if they are the center of someone's world, Scorpios do not fall in and out of love easily or often. Individuals born under the sign of Scorpio are very careful about the people they choose to become romantically involved with because they want a relationship that lasts. It is hard for them to be casual about any relationship. Scorpios set very high standards, and although they are not looking for perfection, they demand honesty, passion, and commitment.

Scorpios are known for being deeply sexual, but because they are often driven to extremes, a Scorpio may, for her own reasons, be celibate for long periods of time. Even though she is happiest when in a satisfying sexual relationship, she prefers being alone to having a series of one-night stands or short-term relationships.

When Scorpio does find the right person, she moves quickly. It may often seem to the people who know her that Scorpio moves too fast in a relationship, but this is very much in her nature. Scorpio is happiest when power, control, and passion all come together. For this reason she is likely to fall in love with someone whose temperament matches hers. This allows the power in a relationship to be balanced, and Scorpio will not be tempted to be the one who runs the relationship.

Finding That Special Someone

Surprisingly, Scorpios may not make a concerted effort to look for a soul mate. Although this sounds unlikely, it relates to their intuitive sense. They have a tendency to believe that true love and attraction are based on destiny, and that if they are meant to meet their true "other half," they will. For them, such meetings may happen at a library, bookstore, planetarium, charity event, or church.

First Dates

Scorpios prefer quiet, intimate venues, especially for something as important as a first date. Yet, because they are not particularly talkative, they may enjoy an atmosphere that is relaxing but does not demand constant conversation. The best choice is to surround them with music at a jazz club, a rock concert, an opera, or even a musical at a dinner theater. Scorpios' deep emotions are stirred by music in ways that words cannot touch. They are a Water sign, so an evening walk on the beach or a sunset stroll by the lake puts them at ease.

Scorpio in Love

Scorpios are deeply attached to their loved ones. They can be possessive and dominating, but they are also very faithful when they are in love. They believe that fidelity is one of the most important elements in a relationship.

Scorpios aspire to a level of purity that is hard for the other Sun signs to even imagine. Scorpios attract their loved ones like a magnet, and have an almost psychic insight into the motives and secrets of their mates. Anyone who dislikes someone knowing their secrets should stay away from Scorpios.

Undying Love

They may be known as the sexiest sign, but there is absolutely nothing trivial or superficial about the way Scorpios approach love. They believe in sincerity and honesty. However, there is also a negative side to their intensity, which can sometimes lead them to be obsessed by their love for someone. Separation from the one she loves isn't only unpleasant; it is actually painful. It can be hard for a Scorpio to keep from being wildly jealous if she feels that someone is trying to steal the affections of the one she loves.

Expectations in Love

Scorpio expects passion and intensity and absolute faithfulness in her relationships. Although her love life may take on the appearance of a romance novel, this is how Scorpio likes it. She is very demonstrative, and makes her lover feel very special. She expects complete loyalty, and can be the most tender and passionate mate if she feels secure.

Scorpios often rush into having a sexual relationship before they have any other kind of relationship. This dangerous habit it is usually the result of a desire for approval. Because emotional intimacy is so important to them, they sometimes make themselves believe that physical intimacy will suffice.

Scorpios usually keep their feelings and thoughts to themselves, for they are too deep for mere words. However, they do not hesitate to make the perfect comment at the perfect time, especially if it will deflate someone's pompous ego. Scorpios must avoid their tendency to test their lovers against the most extreme of hypothetical circumstances. That can distract them from listening to advice that can help them become more powerful individuals.

What Scorpios Look For

Seriousness and wisdom are two traits that appeal to Scorpios. They like someone with sexual appeal, yet their taste is not likely to reflect the stereotypical image of good looks and sexiness. A quirky sense of humor and a unique perspective on life appeal to them. A Scorpio may often be attracted to someone whom they may feel they have known and loved in a previous lifetime.

If Scorpios Only Knew...

If Scorpios only knew that they were not being judged as harshly as they sometimes judge others, they would relax more and not put so much stress on themselves to succeed in everything they do. Scorpios work very hard to impress other people with their efforts, but the one they want most to impress is themselves. This is complicated by the fact that they feel they are being graded, perhaps unable to achieve the high standards they, and others, expect. They should know that it is no sin to take a day off once in a while to rest and regroup.

Marriage

Scorpio is loyal to his partner and does anything for her. But the person who marries a typical Scorpio must realize that Scorpio expects to dominate the partnership. The Scorpio has to feel proud of his partner and her skills, and he goes to great ends to enable his partner to achieve her ambitions, too. Scorpio shrewdness is a vital asset in any partnership.

A Scorpio who accepts orders from a partner does so for a particular reason. For example, if money or future progress is the reward, Scorpio acquiesces. Scorpio waits for as long as it takes to achieve the results he wants. It is unlikely for Scorpio and his partner to have a marriage without extreme ups and downs, and intense highs and lows.

Scorpio's Opposite Sign

Taurus is Scorpio's complementary sign, and even though the two share the virtues of loyalty, determination, and passion, they are very different in other ways. Taurus has the temerity to bring Scorpio down to earth with her own commonsense approach to living, and although Taurus is attracted to Scorpio's mysterious charm, she isn't overwhelmed by it. Scorpio is able to bring out the spiritual potential in Taurus' earthy nature, while Taurus teaches Scorpio how to be patient and sociable.

Pairing Up

In general, if people display the characteristics typical of their sign, intimate relationships between a Scorpio and another individual can be described as follows:

Scorpio with Scorpio
Harmonious; two souls bound together by passion and honor

Scorpio with Sagittarius
Harmonious, with Sagittarius' sense of fun a positive factor

Scorpio with Capricorn
Harmonious, if Scorpio knows how to light Capricorn's fire

Scorpio with Aquarius
Difficult, but a brilliant match when it works

Scorpio with Pisces
Harmonious; one of the most intense and passionate love matches

Scorpio with Aries
Turbulent; an almost impossible meld unless love finds a way

Scorpio with Taurus
Difficult, yet Taurus can bring Scorpio down to earth

Scorpio with Gemini
Turbulent, because free-spirited Gemini won't be controlled

Scorpio with Cancer
Harmonious; a romance of
great intensity

Scorpio with Leo
Difficult, but exciting as lovers

Scorpio with Virgo
Harmonious, so long as Scorpio
doesn't try to dominate Virgo

Scorpio with Libra
Harmonious, thanks to Libra's
amiability and poise

If Things Don't Work Out

Scorpio has been known to harbor anger, resentment, and even revenge fantasies when a relationship ends. It can be very hard for Scorpio to see her own part in a romantic or marital failure, and even harder for her to move past the bad feelings it creates. However, a spiritually evolved Scorpio comes to understand that she must forgive herself and her partner for whatever went wrong in the relationship if she wishes to move on to better things.

Scorpio at Work

Sometimes Scorpios may have to be a bit cold-blooded to make sure that they get what is coming to them. They can be ruthlessly competitive about promotions, raises, and projects at work. Scorpios should not openly confront anyone unless they are absolutely sure that they have the resources on all levels to handle what could be used against them. Power struggles could get quite intense.

Scorpios may want to be less confrontational and work their will beneath the surface and behind the scenes. Scorpios usually benefit from being as secretive and subtle as they can be, but they should not let these traits undermine their effectiveness.

Scorpios should not reveal all of their dreams to just anyone. Scorpios need to learn how to use other people's money and resources to their advantage. If Scorpios have been working hard to obtain the trust of those they work with, they should ask for more responsibility, including handling other people's money. If that happens, Scorpios must treat it as a sacred trust.

Typical Occupations

Scorpios are well suited for work in banking, asset management, recycling, estate planning, detective work, the mantic arts (astrology, the tarot, and other occult subjects), magic, and matters related to sex. Police work, espionage, the law, physics, and psychology are all attractive professions for Scorpio.

Any occupation in which Scorpios feel important and that offers the opportunity to investigate and analyze complex problems will satisfy them. Their inner intensity and outer focus can result in the concentration of a surgeon, pathologist, or scientist. Any profession in which research or dealing with the solving of mysteries is present appeals to Scorpios. Their secretive natures make them natural detectives. They are also likely to succeed in any profession where detailed research is required.

They may be pharmacists, under-takers, insurers, market analysts, or members of the armed services. They can also excel as writers, journalists, and orators. They succeed because they know how to communicate the power of their convictions. Always drawn to extremes, Scorpios do very well working by themselves, or with many people in a large organization.

Details, Details

People born during the time of Scorpio function best in their day-to-day responsibilities when they use their keen intuition as an aid to handling details. They can get to the heart of the matter without regard for diplomacy. Solving mysteries is their talent, and they can get to the root of any problem, human or mechanical. Scorpios enjoy putting together the "clues" they discover from listening to others to solve mysteries about people's motives and actions at work.

Scorpios are very hard workers and are unlikely to see any part of a task as being beneath them or their capabilities. Because they are not very talkative or apt to become involved in social cliques, it should not be assumed that they don't have good teamwork skills. A Scorpio is never too ego-centric to feel as if her contribution to a project must be major in order to fulfill an important role.

The penetrating gaze of a Scorpio is unlikely to miss any detail. Whether she is dealing with figures, outlines, or notes, she peruses the material to see how all the facts fit together. A Scorpio does not forget and usually does not forgive.

Behavior and Abilities at Work

In the workplace, a typical Scorpio:

- is relentless about completing a task

- appears to be confident in all situations

- may not work well as part of a group

- knows the importance of projects

- senses the moods and problems around him

- excels as a team leader

- is willing to put in extra effort on tough tasks

- is loyal and productive

Scorpio As Employer

A typical Scorpio boss:

- demands total loyalty
- helps people he likes
- knows how to get to the heart of the matter
- is secretive about his motives
- confronts a crisis directly
- is concerned if a crisis arises
- makes employees feel like part of a team
- can be ruthless

Scorpio As Employee

A typical Scorpio employee:

- is tenacious, yet calm

- does not waste time

- focuses on what she wants to achieve

- goes after what she wants

- won't accept failure till all attempts to succeed are exhausted

- is intense and career minded

- contributes extra time and effort

- is loyal and efficient

- works overtime when needed

Scorpio As Coworker

The person who works with a Scorpio can expect a passionate drive and unwavering loyalty, along with competitiveness and a dedication to success. The desks and offices of Scorpios are usually clean and neat, with equipment that helps them do their jobs better: reference books, software, and motivational CDs. They are shrewd analysts. Scorpios can work very hard, and they often provide an air of quiet confidence in a business.

Money

Scorpios are inclined to receive awards or enter contests where their ability to discover or even just plain guess secrets wins them a prize. Scorpios are drawn to make money on subjects that have a magical, mystical, or detective theme about them. They might also receive gifts from others in the form of grants, scholarships, and inheritances. Scorpios should plan their estate or set up a trust fund—nothing lasts forever, and it is important that Scorpios plan for the transfer of resources after they leave this world.

Scorpios should be of a single mind about their desire to make money. A negative attitude towards wealthy people could sabotage efforts to become successful. However, they should take great care that they do not attempt to use their money as a means of power, because this always becomes a negative issue for them.

At Home

Scorpios often find it hard to relax. Many Scorpios try to relax by continuing to work, because of the intense pressure they put on themselves to finish everything before leaving for that much-needed rest. Their best policy is to have an alternative interest or hobby that they can pursue with passion, thus giving them relaxation from their main work.

Behavior and Abilities at Home

Scorpio typically:

* expresses herself with color

* is concerned about house security

* is gentle with the sick

* is protective

* guards her privacy

* likes subtle, quiet lighting

* enjoys lounging in underwear or lingerie

Leisure Interests

Scorpios pursue even their leisure interests at an intensity and depth of feeling that other signs would expect to feel about politics, or religion. They don't know the meaning of "it doesn't matter if you win or lose; it's how you play the game." Scorpios enjoy doing things that other people might find too risky or emotionally draining.

The typical Scorpio enjoys the following pastimes:

- browsing through flea markets and thrift shops

- reading detective and mystery novels

- researching ancient civilizations

- studying psychology

- competitive sports

- any game that requires shrewd tactics

Scorpio Likes

- being home
- sex
- intimacy
- privacy
- mysteries
- secrets
- money
- powerful people

Scorpio Dislikes

- shallow relationships
- feeling exposed
- revealing too much
- people who know more than they do
- too many compliments
- having to trust a stranger
- mysteries they can't solve
- ambivalence
- demeaning jobs

The Secret Side of Scorpio

Scorpio is all about secrets. Inside a typical Scorpio is a person who is so guarded that the secrets of Scorpio usually remain secret. All Scorpios like to keep their true nature as hidden as possible. They feel vulnerable to questions about their thoughts and behavior, and for this reason they may choose to stay away from other people born under their Sun sign who are likely to penetrate their emotional armor. Scorpio exercises power through emotion, intellect, and instinct.

Pluto ♀

Pluto is the planet of power and transformation. It symbolizes the part of people that wants to get and use power of every kind. It is the planet of extremes, and so it rules people's personal power to do good, but it also rules power struggles, gangsters, dictators, and the terrible things that happen when people try to make themselves powerful at the expense of others. Pluto is associated with the mysteries of life, magic, sex, and, the ultimate transformation, death. It is also associated with resurrection, whether it be renovating a home, getting cosmetic surgery, or bringing back into a person's life something he thought was long gone. It represents the unconscious mind, invisible yet powerful enough to produce compulsions and obsessions seemingly beyond an individual's control. Like Pluto, their purpose is to help people become aware of what needs to be eliminated from their lives and to help them do so.

Bringing Up a Young Scorpio

Scorpio children are usually active, quick to learn, and intelligent. They have a deep and relentless curiosity that demands to be satisfied. They should be gently guided away from too much interest in forbidden areas, as they have a tendency to be fascinated by everything that is hidden and mysterious. Understanding the rights and needs of others is an important lesson for young Scorpios. In this way Scorpio children learn to forgive the hurts and mishaps of everyday life.

The best way to show love to a Scorpio child is to always be loyal and to make it possible for her to follow an interest in science, medicine, engineering, sports, or literature. Scorpio children who are not kept busy can become sullen, brooding over imagined slights from siblings or other children at school. At times a Scorpio child may feel like an outsider, so it is up to her parents to make her realize that everyone feels that way at times and it is simply a part of life.

A private space is essential for all Scorpio children—someplace where they can be alone and undisturbed. It could be a room of their own or just a closet. A secret hiding place gives the Scorpio child a sense of security.

Scorpio As a Parent

* demands obedience

* is strict and stubborn

* is serious about rules

* keeps children active and involved

* enjoys participating in her child's interests

* can be overprotective

* cares passionately about the family

* finds it hard to admit to a mistake

The Scorpio Child

The typical Scorpio child:

- is very possessive of toys and belongings

- may have an imaginary playmate

- holds her fears inside

- is cautious with strangers

- is a good little detective

- enjoys a contest and likes to win

- learns from mistakes

❈ can be a discipline problem

❈ is loyal to family and friends

❈ gets revenge if crossed

❈ gets along well with adults

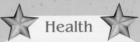

Health

Scorpios are quite often physically strong and enjoy good health. However, some Scorpio individuals do have a tendency to put on weight in later life. Known as the sexiest sign, Scorpios need to release their stress and tension with lovemaking. Their emotions run very deep and their physical needs are great. Nose and throat problems, bladder disorders, and problems with the reproductive organs

are the most common
Scorpio illnesses. People born
under this sign benefit from taking
antioxidants. Scorpios have amazing
recuperative powers, and though they
are rarely ill, they are likely to recover
speedily when they are.

FAMOUS SCORPIOS

Marie Antoinette

Richard Burton

Prince Charles

Hillary Rodham Clinton

Christopher Columbus

Leonardo DiCaprio

Sally Field

Jodie Foster

Bill Gates

Whoopi Goldberg

Goldie Hawn

Grace Kelly

Robert F. Kennedy

Vivien Leigh

Joni Mitchell

Demi Moore

Mike Nichols

Joaquin Phoenix

Pablo Picasso

Julia Roberts

Theodore Roosevelt

Meg Ryan

Carl Sagan

Sam Shepard

Ted Turner

About the Authors

Internationally known self-help author
Monte Farber's inspiring guidance and
empathic insights impact everyone he
encounters. Amy Zerner's exquisite one-
of-a-kind spiritual couture creations and
collaged fabric paintings exude her pro-
found intuition and deep connection
with archetypal stories and healing energies. Together, they have built The
Enchanted World of Amy Zerner and
Monte Farber: books, card decks, and

oracles that have helped millions discover their own spiritual paths.

Their best-selling titles include The Chakra Meditation Kit, The Enchanted Tarot, The Instant Tarot Reader, The Psychic Circle, Karma Cards, The Truth Fairy, The Healing Deck, True Love Tarot, Animal Powers Meditation Kit, The Breathe Easy Deck, The Pathfinder Psychic Talking Board, and Gifts of the Goddess Affirmation Cards.

For further information, please visit:
www.TheEnchantedWorld.com